GREEK ISLAND MYTHS

NAXOS
THESEUS AND ARIADNE

JILL DUDLEY

PUT IT IN YOUR POCKET SERIES
ORPINGTON PUBLISHERS

Published by
Orpington Publishers

Cover design and origination by
Creeds, Bridport, Dorset
01308 423411

Printed and bound in the UK by
Creeds

ISBN: 978-0-9934890-9-9

NAXOS

THESEUS AND ARIADNE

Naxos, famous for its pure white marble and wine, is one of the more beautiful islands in the Cyclades group. Chora, its main port, is picturesque with its maze of marble-flagged and vaulted alleyways winding their way between flat-roofed houses which climb the hillside to a massive stone-built *kastro* (a Venetian castle) on the summit. There are Venetian mansions also with stone-carved heraldic coats-of-arms above their portals.

What draws the eye of those arriving by ferry-boat – and it is the island's major landmark which stands supreme close to the port – is the Portara. The Portara means 'great doorway' and consists of two monumental white marble uprights joined by a lintel; it is all that remains of a temple which was begun in 530 B.C. but never completed. The ruins stand on the small offshore islet of Palatia near to where the ferry-boats dock. Nowadays the islet is joined to Chora by a long causeway and is easily reached on foot.

After Theseus killed the Minotaur on Crete,* helped by Ariadne, the beautiful daughter of King Minos, they ran away together to Naxos and lived on this islet of Palatia. At some stage Dionysos, god of wine and drama, ordered Theseus in a dream to leave Naxos because he wanted Ariadne for himself. Since Dionysos is said to have married Ariadne, and as he was also patron god of Naxos, many scholars believe that the Portara was part of a temple begun in honour of him. An alternative legend has it that Theseus grew tired of Ariadne and so abandoned her on the islet, and Dionysos found her languishing alone and married her. He gave her a crown which, when she eventually died, was placed in the heavens and became a constellation, the Corona.

Other scholars, however, believe the temple was dedicated to Apollo because it was aligned with Delos, the birthplace of Apollo. When Theseus obeyed the command of Dionysos to leave, he sailed first to Delos before going on to Athens* where his father, King Aegeas, was awaiting his return. His homecoming, though, turned to tragedy. It had been agreed with his father that, if he was successful in killing the Minotaur, he would return with a white sail hoisted, but if he failed, then the boat would return with a black sail as a sign of his death. On arrival, Theseus forgot to hoist the white sail and King Aegeus, supposing that his son had been killed, cast himself off a cliff into the sea and was drowned – hence the name the Aegean sea.

To get back to Naxos and the great Portara. The temple was

the dream of the tyrant Lygdamis at a time when Naxos was flourishing. He wanted it to surpass all other temples in size and magnitude, but his plans came to nothing when Naxos went to war with the island of Samos. We can be certain that there was originally more than just the entranceway, because there are signs of a stylobate (a stepped platform on which columns stand), with scattered remains of column drums and marble blocks lying about. A peacock-blue sea surrounds it, lapping against slate-grey rocks.

In Homer's *Hymn to Dionysos* the god was captured by pirates. They had spotted him on mainland Greece disguised as a handsome youth and, thinking him the son of a king, seized and bound him. Much to their consternation the bindings would not hold and, worse still, wine began to flood the deck, a vine grew from the sail heavy with bunches of grapes, and ivy began to twine around the mast. Their captive then turned into a lion and roared at the crew who by now realized the handsome youth must be a god. Eventually they were so terror-stricken they dived overboard, except for the helmsman whom Dionysos commanded to sail on to Naxos where he made him his priest.

When Christianity came to the island, the pagan story regarding bringing the vine to Naxos was discarded and instead it became the work of a saint – St. Dionysios who came from Mt. Olympus. The saint was seated on a rock one day when he spotted a plant growing at his feet; it looked so beautiful that he dug it up. He was on his way to Naxos and, to keep the plant from withering, he put it in the leg-bone of a bird. The plant loved it and outgrew the bird's leg-bone, so the saint next placed it in the bone of a lion. Then, outgrowing that, it was finally placed in the bone of an ass. When he arrived in Naxos, the saint planted it and it bore magnificent bunches of grapes. Whether it was the pagan god, or the Christian saint who brought the vine, remains a mystery. What is certain, however, is that Naxos became famous for its wine.

Today it is possible to visit an ancient sanctuary of Dionysos a little inland south of Chora. It is rectangular, with many broken columns and one with an Ionic capital. What is seen today dates from the fifth century B.C., but earlier temples built successively on the same site date as far back as the ninth century B.C. Somewhat unusually it is aligned towards a nearby river because it was regarded as the source of energy. Most temples face the rising sun. The river, however, flooded, and when it was in full spate it destroyed the temple which consequently had to be rebuilt. With the coming of Christianity, the temple was pulled down and a church dedicated to St. George was constructed on the site. But that too was destroyed by the river when it burst its banks. The church was again rebuilt, but this time a few miles away on higher ground.

The god Dionysos was born in a very strange way. Zeus, supreme god of the ancient world, god of the heavens and often known as the 'cloud-gatherer', was enamoured of a mortal woman Semele. When Zeus' wife, Hera, learned of the affair, she persuaded Semele to ask Zeus to reveal himself to her in his full glory as a god. This she did, with the disastrous consequence that it reduced her to a cinder. Zeus, however, saved the embryo of his unborn child, and placed it in his thigh until the infant Dionysos was ready to be born.

A second version of the birth of Dionysos gives him another mother. This was Kore, or Persephone, the daughter of Demeter, goddess of corn. In this story Zeus is still the father, but his wife Hera is so angry, that she had the child torn limb from limb by the Titans. The heart of Dionysos alone was saved and was given by Zeus to Semele to swallow, whereupon Dionysos became known as Dionysos the 'twice born'. The story signifies the dark forces of nature. Further south from the temple of Dionysos, within easy driving distance, is a temple of Demeter, near to the village of Apo Sangri. It is an impressive edifice with soaring white columns in Naxian marble rising from its stylobate.

The Naxians like to think that Zeus, supreme god of all the Olympians, grew up on Naxos; there is a cave on Mount Zas which claims the honour of once being his home, which can be reached from the village of Filoti. But Crete also claims this honour with its Idaion cave. The walk to the cave here on Naxos is panoramic, with views to the sea across a plateau filled with silver-grey olive trees, pierced here and there with the bottle-green shafts of cypress trees. As you walk along the goat-track, the plateau narrows to become a gorge. The mountain crags across the gorge are of white marble which gleam in the sunlight. The cave itself is of no great significance apart from its connection with Zeus.

A worthwhile drive takes you to Flerio where there is a *kouros,* a giant recumbent figure of a young male which has lain in the same spot for over two thousand five hundred years. There are several *kouroi* on Naxos. This one is on private property, though visitors are welcome to view it. It lies just inside an open gateway against a stone wall – a male nude nearly six metres long. Some believe the figure was an intended statue of Apollo, others that it was Theseus, while still more say it was Dionysos.

The names bring you back to the story of Theseus and Ariadne who lived and loved on their islet of Palatia where the great marble Portara makes its impact. By day it gleams white against the blue sky, but in the evening light with the setting sun it glows a roseate hue. It is the first thing seen as you arrive by ferry-boat, and the last thing before you round the promontory and sail away to your next island.

Denotes a separate booklet on the subject.

FAMILY TREE OF THE GODS AND GODDESSES

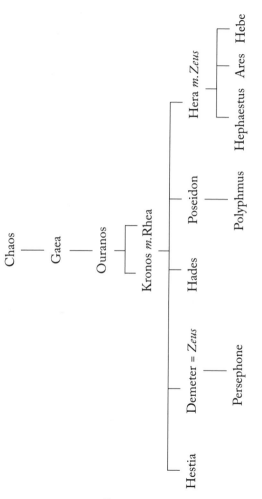

Chaos — Gaea — Ouranos — Kronos *m.* Rhea

Hestia | Demeter = *Zeus* | Hades | Poseidon | Hera *m.* Zeus

Persephone

Polyphmus

Hephaestus Ares Hebe

THE IMMORTAL GODS BORN OF ZEUS BY MORTAL WOMEN

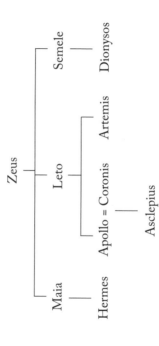

Zeus

Maia — Hermes

Leto
Apollo = Coronis — Artemis
Asclepius

Semele — Dionysos

GLOSSARY OF GODS AND GODDESSES

APOLLO – Son of Zeus and the Titaness Leto. He was twin brother of Artemis, and god of medicine, music, archery and prophecy.

DEMETER – Demeter, goddess of corn, and patroness of agriculture.

DIONYSOS – God of wine and drama. Son of Zeus and the mortal woman Semele.

HERA – Wife and sister of Zeus, and goddess of women and marriage.

KORE – See Persephone.

PERSEPHONE – Daughter of Demeter, sometimes referred to as Kore. When still a young girl she was abducted by Hades and dragged screaming down to his kingdom in the underworld. With Zeus' intervention she was allowed back up to her mother for eight months of the year and returned to Hades for the other four.

TITANS – The offspring of Ouranos (often spelt Uranus, the heavens) and Gaea (the earth). There were said to be twelve of them, six sons and six daughters. Kronos was one of the sons, and Rhea one of the daughters. These two had six children amongst whom were Demeter, Hades, Hera and Zeus.

ZEUS – Son of Kronos and Rhea. He was god of the heavens, and supreme god of the ancient world having deposed his father.

MORE FROM THE
PUT IT IN YOUR POCKET SERIES
GREEK MYTHS

TROJAN WAR
THE JUDGEMENT OF PARIS
HELEN
KING AGAMEMNON
ACHILLES
THE WOODEN HORSE
ODYSSEUS

SACRED SITES
ATHENS – THE ACROPOLIS
CORINTH – ST. PAUL AND THE GODDESS OF LOVE
DELPHI – THE ORACLE OF APOLLO
ELEUSIS – DEMETER AND KORE
EPIDAURUS – CENTRE OF HEALING
OLYMPIA – THE OLYMPIC GAMES

ALSO BY JILL DUDLEY

YE GODS! (TRAVELS IN GREECE)

YE GODS! II (MORE TRAVELS IN GREECE)

LAP OF THE GODS (TRAVELS IN CRETE
AND THE AEGEAN ISLANDS)